I AM KIND

Rourke
Educational Media

A Division of
Carson
Dellosa
Education.

MARLA CONN

Photo Glossary

 **dog**

 **family**

 **friend**

 **myself**

 **neighbor**

 **teacher**

I am kind to my **family.**

family

I am kind to my **teacher**.

I am kind to my **neighbor.**

neighbor

9

I am kind to my **dog**.

dog

I am kind to my **friend.**

13

I am kind to **myself.**

myself

15

Activity

1. Go back to the story with a reading partner. Discuss how each child shown is kind.

2. Brainstorm ways to be kind in home communities and school communities.

3. Why is kindness important to a community?

4. Use your ideas to make a chart on a separate sheet of paper.

Ways we are kind at home	Ways we are kind at school

5. Draw a picture showing how you are kind at home and at school.

CPSIA information can be obtained
at www.ICGtesting.com
Printed in the USA
BVHW061705250522
637513BV00001B/8